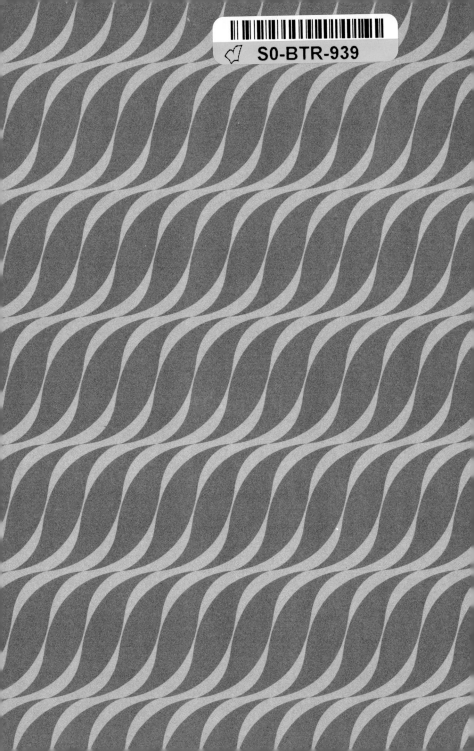

GREAT GARLIC RECIPES

Consulting Editor:
Valerie Ferguson

Contents

Introduction

Glorious garlic—it is difficult to imagine how dull our meals must have been without it. Ancient civilizations such as those of Egypt and Rome were far ahead of us in their appreciation of its many properties, and it has long been vital to the cuisine of continental Europe. Garlic adds a special touch to a wide range of savory dishes: from soups, salads and vegetables to fish, poultry and meat. It can be used raw or lightly cooked to dominate deliciously, or as an ingredient in a slow-cooked casserole, when it will subtly increase the depth of flavor of the dish without being obtrusive. Roasted, it becomes mild and sweet-tasting.

As well as being good for our taste buds, garlic is beneficial to health. It lowers blood cholesterol, thus helping to prevent heart disease. Raw garlic contains a powerful antibiotic and there is evidence that it fights against cancer and strokes, and aids the absorption of vitamins.

So do yourself a favor and try some of the great garlic ideas in this book, which offers recipes for appetizers, snacks, everyday meals and dishes suitable for entertaining, not forgetting, of course, the needs of vegetarians. You will soon be convinced of garlic's star quality.

Types of Garlic

There are numerous varieties of garlic, from the large "elephant" garlic to small, tight bulbs.

The papery skin surrounding each garlic clove can be white, pink or purple. Color makes no difference to taste, but the particular attraction of the large, purple bulbs is that they make a beautiful display in the kitchen.

As a general rule, the smaller the garlic bulb, the stronger it is likely to be. However, most garlic sold at stores is not classified in either shape or form (unless it is elephant garlic), and in practice you will simply pick up whatever you need, either loose, in bunches or on strings.

Garlic grown in a hot climate is likely to be the most pungent, and fresh new garlic has a subtle mild flavor that is particularly good if it is to be used raw—for example, in salads and for dressings.

Buying & Storing
Garlic bulbs should be firm and round with clear, papery skins. Avoid any that are beginning to sprout. Garlic bulbs keep well stored in a cool, dry place; if the air is damp they will sprout, and if it is too warm the cloves will eventually turn to gray powder.

White Garlic
This variety of garlic has a papery, silky skin. A single bulb consists of 8 to 10 plump cloves.

Purple Garlic
These bulbs are valued for their juiciness and long-keeping qualities. The skin may be pink, violet or purple.

Elephant Garlic
A large variety, which is the mildest of all and can be cooked as a vegetable. Its flavor is delicate enough to use raw, but it is also very good roasted.

Smoked Garlic

This has only recently become available and adds a delicate smoked flavor to fish and chicken dishes. It also tastes delicious when roasted and spread on hot toast.

Pickled Garlic

Available at delicatessens and some specialty stores, this comes in jars of either whole bulbs or separate cloves and is very pungent. It is easy to make at home.

Pickled whole garlic

Garlic Pepper & Salt

These products, as their name implies, combine garlic with seasoning. Use in dressings, casseroles, soups or salads.

Garlic pepper

Garlic salt

Garlic Purée

Convenient if fresh garlic is not on hand, but not as flavorful as homemade.

Dried Garlic

Available minced, chopped, powdered and in granules. In its dehydrated form, it is almost odorless, but when rehydrated the flavor is good. These forms of garlic are useful for adding to sauces, curries, soups, stews, salads, chutneys, pickles and relishes.

Garlic-bread Seasoning

A useful seasoning to make quick garlic butter, which can be spread on French bread before baking. Garlic butter can also be melted on hot, cooked vegetables, broiled meat and fish. Combined with fresh basil, salt and olive oil, the seasoning makes a tasty pistou to add to soups.

Techniques

Chopping Garlic

Don't worry if you don't have a garlic press; try this method, which gives wonderfully juicy results.

1 Break off the clove of garlic, place the flat-side of a large knife on top and strike with your fist. Remove all the papery outer skin. Begin by finely chopping the clove.

2 Sprinkle on a little table salt and, using the flat-side of a large knife blade, work the salt into the garlic, until the clove softens and releases its juices. Use as needed.

For very finely crushed garlic, use a garlic press.

Pulping Garlic

If you frequently use pulped garlic, it makes sense to prepare a sizeable batch and store in the refrigerator or freezer until needed. Freezing will not affect the strength of flavor.

1 Separate the garlic into cloves and peel off the paper skin.

2 Process the whole cloves in a food processor or blender.

3 Freeze in ice-cube trays kept specially for the purpose. Put 1 teaspoon in each compartment, freeze, remove from the tray and store in the freezer in a plastic bag. Alternatively, store in an airtight container in the refrigerator for 4–6 weeks.

Basic Recipes

Garlic & Herb Butter

This butter can be prepared ahead and either chilled or frozen until needed. To freeze, wrap in plastic wrap and then in aluminum foil. The butter can be used straight from the freezer.

Makes ½ cup

INGREDIENTS
½ cup unsalted butter
1–2 garlic cloves, chopped
2 tablespoons finely chopped fresh parsley
salt and freshly ground black pepper

1 Place the butter in a mixing bowl and beat with a wooden spoon or electric mixer until soft. Add the chopped garlic, parsley and season to taste with salt and pepper. Blend together until smooth.

2 Place the blended butter on a large sheet of waxed paper and shape it into a roll. Keep the butter and your hands cool while you do this. Wrap up the roll in the paper and chill until firm. Unwrap it and cut into rounds.

Garlic Oil

This oil takes on the delicious flavor of fresh garlic and is invaluable for enlivening salad dressings and sauces and for sautéeing. If the oil solidifies in the refrigerator, soften at room temperature.

1 Trim the root ends off the garlic cloves. Bang them with the back of a knife to loosen the skin. Peel them using your fingers.

2 Hold the garlic cloves, one at a time, between thumb and finger and, using the back of a heavy knife near the handle, crush the cloves by pressing down heavily on a cutting board.

3 Place the crushed garlic in a screw-top jar. Add the olive oil and put the lid on the jar. Store the oil for up to 2 weeks in the refrigerator.

COOK'S TIP: Keeping garlic in oil does not have a preservative effect, and bacteria may form if it is kept too long. Do not keep the oil for longer than 2 weeks.

Garlic, Chickpea & Spinach Soup

A generous amount of garlic brings a good flavor to this creamy soup of mild-tasting vegetables.

Serves 4

INGREDIENTS

2 tablespoons olive oil
4 garlic cloves, crushed
1 onion, roughly chopped
2 teaspoons ground cumin
2 teaspoons ground coriander
5 cups vegetable stock
12 ounces potatoes, finely chopped
15-ounce can chickpeas, drained
    and rinsed
1 tablespoon cornstarch
⅔ cup heavy cream
2 tablespoons light tahini (sesame seed paste)
7 ounces spinach, shredded
cayenne pepper
salt and freshly ground black pepper

2 Pour in the stock and add the potatoes. Bring to a boil and simmer for 10 minutes. Add the chickpeas and simmer for another 5 minutes or until the potatoes are just tender.

3 Blend together the cornstarch, cream, tahini and plenty of seasoning. Stir into the soup with the spinach. Bring to a boil, stirring, and simmer for another 2 minutes.

1 Heat the oil in a large saucepan and cook the garlic and onion for 5 minutes or until they are softened and golden brown. Stir in the cumin and coriander and cook for 1 minute.

4 Adjust the seasoning to taste. Serve immediately in warmed bowls, sprinkled with a little cayenne pepper.

Garlicky Lentil Soup

The long, slow cooking of this soup ensures a mellow garlic flavor.

Serves 6

INGREDIENTS

1 cup red lentils, rinsed and drained
2 onions, finely chopped
2 large garlic cloves, finely chopped
1 carrot, very finely chopped
2 tablespoons olive oil
2 bay leaves
generous pinch of dried marjoram
   or oregano
6¼ cups vegetable stock
2 tablespoons red wine vinegar
salt and freshly ground black pepper
celery leaves, to garnish
crusty rolls, to serve

1 Put the lentils, onions, garlic, carrot, oil, bay leaves, marjoram or oregano and stock in a large, heavy saucepan. Bring to a boil over medium heat, then lower the heat and simmer gently for 1½ hours, stirring the soup occasionally to prevent the lentils from sticking to the bottom of the pan.

2 Remove the bay leaves and add the red wine vinegar, with salt and pepper to taste. If the soup is too thick at this stage, thin it with a little extra vegetable stock or water.

3 Ladle the soup into warmed bowls, garnish with celery leaves and serve accompanied by crusty rolls.

Spanish Garlic Soup

This simple and satisfying garlicky soup is topped with a lightly cooked egg.

Serves 4

INGREDIENTS
2 tablespoons olive oil
4 large garlic cloves, peeled
4 slices French bread,
    ¼-inch thick
1 tablespoon paprika
4 cups beef stock
¼ teaspoon ground cumin
pinch of saffron threads
4 eggs
salt and freshly ground
    black pepper
chopped fresh parsley,
    to garnish

1 Preheat the oven to 450°F. Heat the oil in a large pan. Add the garlic cloves and cook until golden. Remove from the pan and set aside. Fry the bread in the oil until golden, then remove and set aside.

2 Add the paprika to the pan and fry for a few seconds. Stir in the stock, cumin and saffron, then add the reserved garlic, crushing the cloves with the back of a wooden spoon. Season, then cook for about 5 minutes.

3 Ladle the soup into four ovenproof bowls and break an egg into each. Place a slice of bread on top of each egg and place in the oven for 3–4 minutes. Sprinkle with parsley and serve immediatley.

Mellow Garlic Dip

Two whole bulbs of garlic may seem like a lot but, once cooked, they become sweet and mellow. Serve with breadsticks and chips.

Serves 4

INGREDIENTS
2 whole garlic bulbs
1 tablespoon olive oil
¼ cup mayonnaise
5 tablespoons plain yogurt
1 teaspoon whole-grain mustard
salt and freshly ground black pepper

1 Preheat the oven to 400°F. Separate the garlic cloves, without peeling them, and place them in a small roasting pan.

2 Pour the olive oil over the garlic cloves and turn them with a spoon to coat them evenly. Roast for 20–30 minutes, until the garlic is tender and softened. Remove from the oven and let cool for 5 minutes.

VARIATION: For a low fat version of this dip, use reduced fat mayonnaise and low-fat plain yogurt.

3 Trim off the root end of each roasted garlic clove. Peel the cloves and discard the skins.

4 Place the roasted garlic on a cutting board and sprinkle with salt. Mash with a fork until puréed.

5 Place the garlic purée in a small bowl and stir in the mayonnaise, yogurt and whole-grain mustard.

6 Check and adjust the seasoning, then spoon the dip into a bowl. Cover and chill until ready to serve.

Garlic Mushrooms

A quick and tasty appetizer.

Serves 4

INGREDIENTS
2 tablespoons sunflower oil
2 tablespoons butter
5 scallions, thinly sliced
3 garlic cloves, crushed
6 cups button mushrooms
¾ cup fresh white bread crumbs
1 tablespoon chopped fresh parsley
2 tablespoons lemon juice
salt and freshly ground black pepper

1 Heat the oil and butter in a wok or heavy frying pan. Add the scallions and garlic and stir-fry over medium heat for 1–2 minutes.

2 Add the mushrooms and cook over high heat for 4–5 minutes, stirring and tossing constantly with a spatula or wooden spoon.

3 Stir in the bread crumbs, parsley, lemon juice and seasoning. Stir-fry for a few minutes, until the lemon juice has virtually evaporated and then serve immediately.

Right: Garlic Mushrooms (top);
Roasted Garlic with Croutons

Roasted Garlic with Croutons

Roasted garlic is always a favorite.

Serves 4

INGREDIENTS
2 whole garlic bulbs
3 tablespoons olive oil
3 tablespoons water
sprig of fresh rosemary
sprig of fresh thyme
1 bay leaf
salt and freshly ground black pepper

TO SERVE
olive or sunflower oil, for frying
slices of French bread
¾ cup young goat cheese or soft
    cream cheese
2 teaspoons chopped fresh herbs, such as
    marjoram, parsley and chives

1 Preheat the oven to 375°F. Place the garlic bulbs in a small, ovenproof dish and pour on the oil and water. Add the herbs and season. Cover with aluminum foil. Bake for 45–50 minutes.

2 Heat a little oil in a frying pan and fry the bread on both sides. Blend the cheese with the herbs and place in a serving dish. Cut each garlic bulb in half and open out slightly. Serve on small plates with the croutons and cheese. Each clove should be squeezed out, spread on a crouton and eaten with the cheese.

Artichokes with Green Beans & Garlic Dressing

The strongly flavored garlic dressing complements the artichokes and green beans perfectly in this Mediterranean recipe.

Serves 3–6

INGREDIENTS
8 ounces green beans
3 small globe artichokes
1 tablespoon olive oil
pared zest of 1 lemon
coarse salt, for sprinkling
lemon wedges, to garnish

FOR THE DRESSING
6 large garlic cloves, sliced
2 teaspoons white wine vinegar
1 cup olive oil
salt and freshly ground
   black pepper

1 To make the dressing, put the garlic and vinegar in a blender or mini food processor. With the machine switched on, gradually pour in the olive oil until the mixture is thickened and smooth. Alternatively, crush the garlic into a paste with the vinegar and gradually beat in the oil using a hand whisk. Season with salt and pepper to taste.

2 Cook the beans in boiling water for 1–2 minutes, until slightly softened. Drain well.

3 Trim the artichoke stalks close to the bottom. Cook the artichokes in a large pan of salted water for about 30 minutes or until you can easily pull off a leaf from the bottom. Drain well.

4 Using a sharp knife, halve the artichokes lengthwise. Ease out the hairy choke using a teaspoon.

5 Arrange the artichokes and beans on serving plates and drizzle on the oil. Sprinkle on the lemon zest and season with coarse salt and a little freshly ground pepper.

6 Spoon the dressing into the artichoke hearts and serve warm, garnished with lemon wedges. To eat artichokes, pull the leaves from the bottom one at a time, and use to scoop a little of the dressing. It is the fleshy end of each leaf that is eaten, as well as the "heart" of the artichoke.

COOK'S TIP: Mediterranean baby artichokes are sometimes available and are perfect for this kind of salad as, unlike the larger ones, they can be eaten whole. Cook them until just tender, then cut in half to serve.

Cod with Garlic

Mayonnaise with garlic is excellent with baked fish.

Serves 4

INGREDIENTS
4 anchovy fillets, finely chopped
3 tablespoons chopped fresh parsley
6 tablespoons olive oil
4 cod fillets, about 1½ pounds total, skinned
¾ cup fresh bread crumbs
freshly ground black pepper

FOR THE MAYONNAISE
2 garlic cloves, finely chopped
1 egg yolk
1 teaspoon Dijon mustard
¾ cup vegetable oil

1 To make the mayonnaise, put the garlic in a bowl and mash into a paste. Beat in the egg yolk and mustard. Add the oil slowly while beating vigorously with a wire whisk. When the mixture is thick and smooth, season. Cover the bowl and keep cool.

2 Preheat the oven to 400°F. Place the anchovies and the parsley in a bowl and add pepper and 3 tablespoons of the oil. Stir. Place the cod in an oiled ovenproof dish. Spread the anchovy paste on top. Sprinkle with the bread crumbs and the remaining oil. Bake for 20–25 minutes. Serve with the mayonnaise.

Monkfish with Garlic & Thyme

This fish combines well with garlic, tomatoes and olives.

Serves 4

INGREDIENTS
1¼ pounds monkfish fillet, cut into slices
    ½ inch thick
3 tablespoons extra virgin olive oil
½ cup small black olives, pitted
1 large or 2 small tomatoes, seeded
    and diced
1 fresh thyme sprig or 1 teaspoon
    dried thyme,
3 garlic cloves, chopped
salt and freshly ground black pepper
fresh thyme sprigs, to garnish

1 Preheat the oven to 400°F. Heat a nonstick frying pan until quite hot, without oil. Sear the fish quickly on both sides.

2 Spread 1 tablespoon of the olive oil in the bottom of a shallow baking dish. Arrange the fish in one layer with the olives and tomato on top.

3 Sprinkle the fish with thyme, garlic, salt and pepper, and the remaining oil. Bake for 10–12 minutes. Garnish with thyme sprigs and serve.

Right: Cod with Garlic (top);
Monkfish with Garlic & Thyme

Red Snapper with Rosemary & Garlic

Garlic slivers are slipped into slits cut in these simply cooked fish.

Serves 4

INGREDIENTS

4 red snapper, about 10 ounces
   each, cleaned
4 garlic cloves, cut lengthwise into
   thin slivers
5 tablespoons olive oil
2 tablespoons balsamic vinegar
2 teaspoons very finely chopped fresh
   rosemary or 1 teaspoon dried rosemary
freshly ground black pepper
fresh rosemary sprigs and lemon wedges,
   to garnish
coarse sea salt, to serve

1 Cut three diagonal slits in both sides of each fish. Push the garlic slivers into the slits. Place the fish in a single layer in a shallow ovenproof dish. Whisk the oil, vinegar and rosemary, with pepper to taste.

2 Pour the mixture onto the fish, cover and let marinate in a cool place for about 1 hour. Preheat the broiler.

3 Put the fish on the rack of a broiler pan and broil for 5–6 minutes on each side, turning once and brushing with the marinade. Serve hot, sprinkled with coarse sea salt and garnished with fresh rosemary sprigs and lemon wedges.

Fillets of Hake Baked with Garlic

Use the freshest garlic available for this simple fish recipe.

Serves 4

INGREDIENTS
4 hake fillets, about 6 ounces each
1 shallot, finely chopped
2 garlic cloves, thinly sliced
4 fresh thyme sprigs, plus extra to garnish
grated zest and juice of 1 lemon, plus extra
    juice for drizzling
2 tablespoons extra virgin olive oil
salt and freshly ground black pepper

1 Preheat the oven to 350°F. Lay the hake fillets in the bottom of a large roasting pan. Sprinkle the shallot, garlic and thyme on top. Season well with salt and pepper.

2 Drizzle on the lemon juice and oil. Bake for about 15 minutes or until the fish is just cooked through but still firm.

3 Serve immediately, with finely grated lemon zest and garnished with thyme sprigs.

VARIATIONS: If hake is not available, you can substitute cod or haddock fillets. You can also use a mixture of fresh herbs rather than just thyme.

Red Snapper with Garlic, Chili & Ginger Sauce

Gin, chile and garlic add piquancy and spice to a fine fish dish that tastes every bit as good as it looks.

Serves 4

INGREDIENTS
3–3½-pound red snapper, cleaned
2 tablespoons sunflower oil
1 onion, chopped
2 garlic cloves, crushed
¾ cup button mushrooms, sliced
1 teaspoon ground coriander
1 tablespoon chopped fresh parsley
2 tablespoons grated fresh ginger root
2 fresh red chiles, seeded and sliced
1 tablespoon cornstarch
3 tablespoons gin
1¼ cups chicken or vegetable stock
salt and freshly ground
    black pepper

FOR THE GARNISH
1 tablespoon sunflower oil
6 garlic cloves, sliced
1 lettuce heart, finely shredded
1 bunch cilantro, tied with
    red raffia

1 Preheat the oven to 375°F. Grease an ovenproof dish large enough to hold the fish. Make several diagonal cuts on one side of the fish.

2 Heat the oil in a frying pan and cook the onion, garlic and mushrooms for 2–3 minutes. Stir in the ground coriander and chopped parsley. Season with salt and pepper.

3 Spoon the onion mixture into the cavity of the fish, then lift it carefully into the dish. Pour in enough cold water to cover the bottom of the dish. Sprinkle the ginger and chiles onto the fish, cover and bake for 30–40 minutes, basting occasionally. Remove the cover for the last 10 minutes.

4 Carefully lift the fish onto a warmed serving dish and keep hot. Transfer the cooking juices into a pan.

5 Blend the cornstarch and gin in a small bowl and stir into the cooking juices. Pour in the stock. Bring to a boil and cook gently for 3–4 minutes or until thickened, stirring constantly. Taste and adjust the seasoning as necessary, then pour into a sauce boat.

6 To make the garnish, heat the oil in a small pan and stir-fry the sliced garlic and shredded lettuce over high heat until crisp. Spoon alongside the snapper. Place the cilantro bouquet on the other side. Serve immediately with the sauce.

Roast Monkfish with Garlic & Fennel

The flavor of garlic really penetrates the fish in this recipe, which is impressive enough to serve at a dinner party. You can ask the fishmonger to fillet the fish for you, but it is simple to do yourself.

Serves 4

INGREDIENTS
2½-pound monkfish tail
8 garlic cloves
1 tablespoon olive oil
2 fennel bulbs, sliced
grated zest and juice of 1 lemon
1 bay leaf, plus extra to garnish
salt and freshly ground
   black pepper

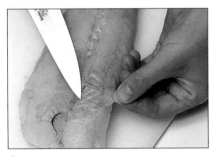

1 Preheat the oven to 425°F. With a filleting knife, cut off the thin membrane covering the outside of the fish.

VARIATION: For a more colorful effect, use eight thickly shredded radicchio leaves instead of the fennel bulbs.

2 Cut along one side of the central bone to remove the fillet. Repeat on the other side. Tie the fillets together with string.

3 Peel and slice the garlic cloves and make incisions in the fish flesh. Place the garlic slices in the incisions.

4 Heat the oil in a large, heavy saucepan, add the fish and fry briefly over high heat to seal on all sides.

5 Place the fish in a roasting dish with the fennel, lemon juice, seasoning and bay leaf. Roast for about 20 minutes or until the fish is just cooked through. Serve immediately, garnished with bay leaves and grated lemon zest.

Shrimp with Garlic Bread Crumbs

Fresh shrimp are a delight to eat, especially when smothered in garlic butter and topped with fresh golden bread crumbs. Halve the recipe for appetizer portions.

Serves 4

INGREDIENTS
32 medium shrimp
1½ cups butter, softened
8 garlic cloves, chopped
2 tablespoons chopped
 fresh parsley
4 scallions, finely chopped
1 tablespoon whole-grain mustard
2 cups fresh white bread crumbs
freshly ground black pepper
fresh parsley sprigs,
 to garnish
brown bread, to serve

2 Preheat the oven to 400°F. Place the butter, garlic, parsley, scallions, mustard and black pepper in a bowl. Beat until blended.

3 Divide the peeled shrimp among four ovenproof dishes. Divide the butter among them and spread it onto the shrimp with the back of a knife. Sprinkle with the bread crumbs.

4 Place the dishes in the oven and cook for 15 minutes or until the bread crumbs are golden brown. Garnish with parsley and the unpeeled shrimp, and serve with brown bread.

1 Bring a large pan of water to a boil. Drop in the shrimp. Cook until they float on top of the water. Drain and refresh under cold water, then peel all but four and set aside.

VARIATION: For a spicier version, substitute the scallions with a red chile, seeded and chopped, and use chives instead of parsley.

French-style Chicken with Garlic

Use new garlic—there's no need to peel it if the skin is not papery.

Serves 8

INGREDIENTS
4½ pounds chicken portions
2 tablespoons butter
1 tablespoon olive oil
1 large onion, halved and sliced
3 large garlic bulbs, about 7 ounces,
    separated into cloves and peeled
⅔ cup dry white wine
¾ cup chicken stock
4–5 fresh thyme sprigs
1 small fresh rosemary sprig
3 bay leaves
salt and freshly ground black pepper

1 Preheat the oven to 375°F. Season the chicken. Heat the butter and oil in a flameproof casserole.

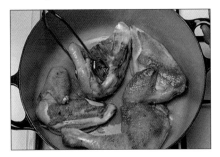

2 Put the chicken skin-side down in the casserole. Fry until browned, turning frequently. Transfer to a plate. Cook in batches if necessary and pour off the fat after browning.

3 Add the onion and garlic to the casserole and cook over medium-low heat, covered, until lightly browned, stirring frequently.

4 Add the wine, bring to a boil and return the chicken to the casserole. Add the stock and herbs and bring back to a boil. Cover and transfer to the oven. Cook for 25 minutes or until the chicken is tender and the juices run clear when the thickest part of the thigh is pierced with a knife.

5 Remove the chicken pieces from the casserole and strain the cooking liquid. Discard the herbs, transfer the solids to a food processor and purée until smooth.

6 Remove any fat from the cooking liquid and return to the casserole. Stir in the garlic and onion purée, return the chicken to the casserole and reheat gently for 3–4 minutes before serving.

Garlicky Spiced Grilled Poussins

The cumin, coriander and garlic coating keeps the poussins moist.

Serves 4

INGREDIENTS
2 garlic cloves, roughly chopped
1 teaspoon ground cumin
1 teaspoon ground coriander
pinch of cayenne pepper
½ small onion, chopped
¼ cup olive oil
½ teaspoon salt
2 poussins
lemon wedges, to garnish

1 Combine the garlic, cumin, coriander, cayenne pepper, onion, olive oil and salt in a blender or food processor. Process to make a paste.

2 Cut the poussins in half lengthwise. Place them skin-side up in a shallow dish and spread with the spice paste. Cover and marinate for 2 hours.

3 Preheat the broiler or prepare a grill. Broil or grill the poussins for 15–20 minutes, turning frequently, until cooked and lightly charred. Serve, garnished with lemon wedges.

Right: Garlicky Spiced Grilled Poussins (top); Chicken with 40 Cloves of Garlic

Chicken with 40 Cloves of Garlic

Long, slow cooking makes the garlic soft and flavors the chicken.

Serves 4–6

INGREDIENTS
½ lemon
fresh rosemary sprigs
3–4½-pound chicken
4 or 5 whole garlic bulbs
¼ cup olive oil
salt and freshly ground black pepper
steamed fava beans and scallions,
    to serve

1 Preheat the oven to 375°F. Place the lemon half and the rosemary sprigs inside the chicken cavity. Separate three or four of the garlic bulbs into cloves and remove the papery husks, but do not peel. Slice the top off the other garlic bulb.

2 Heat the oil in a large, flameproof casserole. Add the chicken, turning it to coat the skin completely. Season and add all the garlic.

3 Cover the casserole with a sheet of foil, then the lid. Place in the oven for 1–1¼ hours, until the chicken is cooked. Serve the chicken with the garlic and cooking juices, accompanied by steamed fava beans and scallions.

Chicken with Garlicky Tomato Sauce

In this tasty dish, the chicken is baked and smothered in a rich, garlicky sauce.

Serves 8

INGREDIENTS
4-pound chicken, cut into
   8 portions
¼ teaspoon chopped fresh thyme
3 tablespoons butter
3 tablespoons vegetable oil
3–4 garlic cloves, crushed
2 onions, finely chopped
½ cup dry sherry
3 tablespoons tomato paste
a few fresh basil leaves
about 2 tablespoons white wine vinegar
generous pinch of sugar
1 teaspoon mild mustard
14-ounce can chopped tomatoes
3¼ cups mushrooms, sliced
salt and freshly ground
   white pepper
fresh basil and thyme leaves,
   to garnish
cooked rice, to serve

1 Preheat the oven to 350°F. Season the chicken portions with salt and pepper and sprinkle with chopped thyme. In a large frying pan, heat the butter and oil and fry the chicken until golden brown on all sides. Remove from the frying pan, place in an ovenproof dish and keep hot.

2 Add the garlic and onion to the frying pan and cook for 2–3 minutes or until just soft.

3 Combine the sherry, tomato paste, basil, vinegar and sugar in a bowl with salt and pepper. Add the mustard and tomatoes. Pour into the frying pan and bring to a boil.

4 Reduce the heat and add the mushrooms. Adjust the seasoning with more sugar or vinegar to taste.

5 Pour the tomato sauce onto the chicken. Bake covered, for 45–60 minutes or until the chicken is cooked thoroughly. Serve immediately on a bed of rice, garnished with basil and thyme leaves.

VARIATION: Replace the cultivated mushrooms with wild mushrooms, if desired, but do make sure that they are cleaned thoroughly before using.

Chicken Thighs with Lemon & Garlic

Whole garlic cloves and slices of lemon are used in this sauce.

Serves 4

INGREDIENTS
2½ cups chicken stock
20 large garlic cloves, peeled
2 tablespoons butter
1 tablespoon olive oil
8 chicken thighs
1 lemon, peeled, pith removed
   and thinly sliced
2 tablespoons all-purpose flour
⅔ cup dry white wine
salt and freshly ground black pepper
chopped fresh parsley or basil, to garnish
bread, to serve

1 Put the stock into a pan and bring to a boil. Add the garlic cloves, cover and simmer gently for 40 minutes.

2 Heat the butter and oil in a frying pan, add the chicken thighs and cook gently on all sides. Transfer them to an ovenproof dish. Preheat the oven to 375°F.

3 Strain the stock and reserve it. Distribute the garlic and lemon slices among the chicken pieces. Add the flour to the fat in the pan in which the chicken was browned, and cook, stirring, for 1 minute.

4 Add the wine, stirring constantly and scraping the bottom of the pan, then add the stock. Cook, stirring, until the sauce has thickened and is smooth. Season with salt and pepper.

5 Pour the sauce onto the chicken, cover and cook for 40–45 minutes or until the chicken is tender.

6 If a thicker sauce is needed, lift out the chicken and reduce the sauce by boiling rapidly until it reaches the desired consistency. Sprinkle on the chopped parsley or basil and serve with thick slices of bread to mop up the juices.

Chicken Cooked in Coconut Milk & Garlic

Garlic, coriander, galangal, lemongrass and kaffir lime leaves flavor the coconut milk to make the sauce for this Indonesian dish.

Serves 4

INGREDIENTS
3–3½-pound chicken or
    4 chicken quarters
4 garlic cloves, peeled
1 onion, sliced
4 macadamia nuts or 8 almonds
1 tablespoon coriander seeds, dry-fried,
    or 1 teaspoon ground coriander
3 tablespoons oil
1-inch piece fresh galangal or ginger root,
    peeled and bruised
2 lemongrass stalks, fleshy
    part bruised
3 kaffir lime leaves
2 bay leaves
1 teaspoon sugar
2½ cups coconut milk
salt
boiled rice and deep-fried onions
    (see Cook's Tip), to serve

2 Grind the garlic, onion, nuts and coriander into a fine paste in a food processor or using a mortar and pestle. Heat the oil in a wok or large frying pan and fry the paste. Do not let it brown.

3 Add the part-cooked chicken together with the galangal or ginger, lemongrass, lime and bay leaves, sugar, coconut milk and salt to taste. Mix well to coat the chicken in the sauce.

COOK'S TIP: To make deep-fried onions, slice 1 pound onions as finely as possible. Spread out thinly on paper towels in an airy place, and let dry for 30 minutes–2 hours. Heat oil in a deep-fryer or wok to 375°F and fry the onions in batches until crisp and golden, turning constantly. Drain well on paper towels and cool.

1 Preheat the oven to 375°F. Cut the chicken into four or eight pieces. Season with salt. Put in an oiled roasting pan and bake for 25–30 minutes. Meanwhile, prepare the sauce.

4 Bring to a boil, reduce the heat and simmer gently for 30–40 minutes, uncovered, until the chicken is tender and the coconut sauce is reduced and thickened. Stir the chicken mixture occasionally during cooking.

5 Just before serving, remove the galangal or ginger and lemongrass. Serve with boiled rice sprinkled with crisp deep-fried onions.

Pork with Marsala & Garlic

Juniper berries mingle with garlic and Marsala to create an inspired sauce.

Serves 4

INGREDIENTS
4 pork cutlets
2 teaspoons balsamic vinegar
8 garlic cloves, unpeeled
1 tablespoon butter
3 tablespoons Marsala
several fresh rosemary sprigs
½ cup dried cèpe or porcini mushrooms,
    soaked in hot water
10 juniper berries, crushed
salt and freshly ground
    black pepper
noodles and green vegetables,
    to serve

1 Brush the pork with 1 teaspoon of the vinegar and season with salt and pepper. Cook the garlic cloves in a small pan of boiling water for 10 minutes. Drain and set aside.

2 Melt the butter in a large frying pan. Add the pork and fry quickly until browned on the underside. Turn the meat over and cook for 1 minute.

3 Add the Marsala, rosemary, mushrooms, 4 tablespoons of the mushroom soaking liquid, the garlic, juniper and remaining vinegar. Simmer gently for about 3 minutes, until the pork is cooked through. Season lightly and serve with noodles and green vegetables of your choice.

Pork & Garlic Sausage Casserole

Garlic sausage lends its unmistakable flavor to this German-style dish.

Serves 6

INGREDIENTS
3 tablespoons sunflower oil
8 ounces lean bacon, diced
1-pound lean shoulder of pork, trimmed and
    cut into 1-inch cubes
1 large onion, sliced
2 pounds potatoes, thickly sliced
1 cup light ale or beer
8 ounces German garlic sausage,
    skinned and sliced
2¼ cups sauerkraut, drained
2 red apples, sliced
1 teaspoon caraway seeds
salt and freshly ground black pepper

1 Preheat the oven to 350°F. Heat
2 tablespoons of the oil in a flameproof
casserole. Fry the bacon for 2–3 minutes,
then lightly brown the cubes of pork.
Remove the meat and set aside.

2 Add the remaining oil to the
casserole and gently cook the onion
for 10 minutes, until soft. Return the
meat to the pan with the potatoes and
ale or beer. Bring to a boil. Cover and
bake for 45 minutes.

3 Stir in the garlic sausage, sauerkraut,
apples and caraway seeds. Season to
taste. Return to the oven and cook for
another 30 minutes. Serve hot.

Lamb Casserole with Garlic & Fava Beans

This recipe, which has a Spanish influence, is based on stewing lamb with garlic and sherry—the addition of fava beans gives color.

Serves 6

INGREDIENTS
3 tablespoons olive oil
3–3½-pound lamb, cut into
    2-inch cubes
1 large onion, chopped
6 large garlic cloves, peeled
1 bay leaf
1 teaspoon paprika
½ cup dry sherry
½ cup beef stock
4 ounces shelled fresh or frozen
    fava beans
2 tablespoons chopped fresh parsley
salt and freshly ground
    black pepper

1 Heat 2 tablespoons of the oil in a large, flameproof casserole. Add half the meat and brown well on all sides. Transfer to a plate. Brown the rest of the meat in the same way and remove from the casserole.

2 Heat the remaining oil in the casserole, add the onion and cook for about 5 minutes, until soft. Return the meat to the casserole.

3 Add the garlic cloves, bay leaf, paprika, sherry and stock. Season with salt and pepper. Bring to a boil, then cover and simmer very gently for 1½–2 hours, until the meat is tender.

4 Add the fava beans about 10 minutes before the end of the cooking time. Stir in the chopped parsley just before serving.

Rack of Lamb with Mustard & Garlic

A scrumptious, crisp crust of bread crumbs coats this tender roast lamb.

Serves 6–8

INGREDIENTS
3 racks of lamb (7–8 ribs each), trimmed of
    fat, bones "French" trimmed
2 or 3 garlic cloves
4 ounces (about 4 slices) white or
    whole-wheat bread, torn into pieces
1½ tablespoons fresh thyme leaves or
    1 tablespoon rosemary leaves
1½ tablespoons Dijon mustard
2 tablespoons olive oil
freshly ground black pepper
fresh rosemary, to garnish
boiled new potatoes, to serve

2 In a food processor fitted with the metal blade, with the machine running, drop the garlic through the feed tube and process until finely chopped. Add the bread, herbs, mustard and a little pepper and process until combined, then slowly pour in the oil in a thin stream.

1 Preheat the oven to 425°F. Trim all the remaining fat from the lamb.

COOK'S TIP: To "French" trim, cut the top 1½ inches of meat from the thin end of the bones and scrape clean.

3 Press the bread crumb mixture onto the meaty side and ends of the lamb, completely covering the surface.

4 Put the racks in a shallow roasting pan and roast for about 25 minutes for medium-rare or 3–5 more minutes for medium (a meat thermometer inserted into the thickest part of the meat should register 135–140°F for medium-rare to medium).

5 Transfer the meat to a carving board or warmed platter. Cut down between the bones to carve into chops. Serve garnished with rosemary and accompanied by new potatoes.

Corsican Beef & Garlic Stew with Macaroni

A rich, slowly cooked stew, well flavored with garlic. Here the gravy is served as a sauce for the accompanying macaroni, in the traditional Corsican way.

Serves 4

INGREDIENTS
½ cup dried mushrooms (cèpes)
6 garlic cloves, peeled
2 pounds stewing beef, cut into
   2-inch cubes
4 ounces lardons, or thick bacon
   cut into strips
3 tablespoons olive oil
2 onions, sliced
1¼ cups dry white wine
2 tablespoons passata
pinch of ground cinnamon
sprig of fresh rosemary
1 bay leaf
2 cups large macaroni
⅔ cup freshly grated
   Parmesan cheese
salt and freshly ground black pepper

1 Soak the dried mushrooms in warm water for 30 minutes. Drain, set the mushrooms aside and reserve the soaking liquid.

2 Cut three of the garlic cloves into thin strips and insert into the pieces of beef by making little slits with a sharp knife. Push the lardons or pieces of bacon into the beef with the garlic. Season the meat with salt and pepper.

3 Heat the oil in a heavy pan, add half the beef and brown well on all sides. Transfer to a plate. Repeat with the remaining beef.

4 Add the sliced onions to the pan and cook until lightly browned. Crush the remaining garlic and add to the onions. Return the meat to the pan.

5 Stir in the wine, passata, mushrooms, cinnamon, rosemary and bay leaf and season with salt and pepper. Cook gently for 30 minutes, stirring often.

6 Strain the mushroom liquid and add to the stew with enough water to cover. Bring to a boil, cover and simmer very gently for 3 hours, until the meat is tender.

7 Cook the macaroni in a large pan of boiling, salted water for 10 minutes, or according to the package instructions, until *al dente*. Lift the pieces of meat out of the gravy and transfer to a warmed serving platter. Drain the pasta and layer in a serving bowl with the gravy and cheese. Serve with the meat.

Spaghettini with Roasted Garlic

The sweet taste of roasted garlic is milder than you would expect.

Serves 4

INGREDIENTS
1 whole garlic bulb
14 ounces fresh or dried spaghettini
½ cup extra virgin olive oil
salt and freshly ground
   black pepper
coarsely shaved Parmesan cheese and
   crusty bread (optional), to serve

1 Preheat the oven to 350°F. Place the whole garlic bulb in a well-oiled baking pan and roast it for 30 minutes.

2 Cook the pasta in a saucepan of boiling salted water according to the instructions on the package, until it is *al dente*.

3 Let the garlic cool, then lay it on its side and slice off the top third of the bulb with a sharp knife.

4 Hold the garlic over a bowl and dig out the flesh from each clove with the point of the knife. When all the flesh has been added to the bowl, pour in the oil and add plenty of black pepper. Mix well.

5 Drain the pasta and return it to the clean pan. Pour in the oil and garlic mixture and toss the pasta vigorously over medium heat until all the strands are thoroughly coated.

COOK'S TIP: Although you can now buy roasted garlic at supermarkets, it is best to roast it yourself for this simple recipe, so that it melts into the olive oil and coats the strands of pasta beautifully.

6 Serve immediately, with shavings of Parmesan passed separately and accompanied by crusty bread to mop up the juices, if desired.

VARIATION: For a fiery finish, sprinkle crushed dried red chiles onto the pasta when tossing it with the oil and garlic.

Feta, Roasted Garlic & Oregano Pizza

A pizza for garlic lovers! Peel the cloves before eating.

Serves 4

INGREDIENTS
1 whole medium garlic bulb
3 tablespoons olive oil
1 medium red bell pepper, quartered
   and seeded
1 medium yellow bell pepper, quartered
   and seeded
2 plum tomatoes
¾ cup feta cheese, crumbled
freshly ground black pepper
1–2 tablespoons chopped fresh oregano,
   to garnish

FOR THE DOUGH
½ teaspoon active dry yeast
pinch of sugar
4 cups all-purpose flour
1 teaspoon salt
2 tablespoons olive oil

1 To make the dough, put 1¼ cups warm water in a measuring cup. Add the yeast and sugar and set aside for 5–10 minutes until frothy.

2 Sift the flour and salt into a large bowl and make a well in the center. Gradually mix in the yeast mixture and oil to make a smooth dough. Knead lightly on a floured surface for about 10 minutes, until smooth and elastic, then set, covered, in a warm place, for 1½ hours to rise.

3 Preheat the oven to 400°F. Break the garlic into cloves, discarding the outer papery leaves. Toss the cloves in 1 tablespoon of the oil, then set aside.

4 Place the red and yellow peppers skin-side up on a baking sheet and broil until the skins are evenly charred. Place in a covered bowl for about 10 minutes, then peel off the skins. Cut the flesh into strips.

5 Put the tomatoes in a bowl and pour in boiling water. Set aside for 30 seconds, then plunge into cold water. Peel, seed and roughly chop the flesh.

6 Divide the dough into four pieces and roll out each one on a lightly floured surface to a 5-inch circle.

7 Place the dough circles well apart on two greased baking sheets, then push up the dough edges to form a thin rim. Brush with half the remaining oil and sprinkle on the chopped tomatoes. Top with the peppers, crumbled feta and garlic cloves. Drizzle on the remaining oil and season with black pepper.

8 Bake the pizzas for 15–20 minutes, until crisp and golden. Garnish with chopped oregano and serve immediately.

VARIATION: Try this pizza with other toppings, such as sun-dried tomatoes, olives and mozzarella.

Zucchini Fritters with Garlic Pistou

The garlic pistou sauce provides a great contrast in flavor and texture to these delicious fritters, which are a specialty of southern France.

Serves 4

INGREDIENTS
1 pound zucchini, grated
⅔ cup all-purpose flour
1 egg, separated
1 tablespoon olive oil
oil, for shallow frying
salt and freshly ground
    black pepper

FOR THE GARLIC PISTOU
½ ounce basil leaves
4 garlic cloves, peeled
1 cup freshly grated
    Parmesan cheese
finely grated zest of 1 lemon
⅔ cup olive oil

1 To make the garlic pistou, crush the basil leaves and garlic, using a mortar and pestle, to make a fairly fine paste. Transfer the paste to a bowl and stir in the grated cheese and lemon zest. Gradually blend in the oil, a little at a time, until combined, then transfer to a small serving dish.

2 Put the grated zucchini in a sieve set over a bowl and sprinkle with plenty of salt. Put a plate with a weight on top. Let sit for 1 hour, then rinse thoroughly. Dry well on paper towels.

3 Sift the flour into a bowl and make a well in the center, then add the egg yolk and oil. Measure 5 tablespoons water and add to the bowl.

4 Stir the zucchini into the batter. Whisk the egg white until stiff, then fold into the batter.

5 Heat ½ inch oil in a frying pan. Add spoonfuls of batter to the oil and fry for 2 minutes, until golden. Drain the fritters on paper towels and keep warm while frying the rest. Serve with the pistou.

Garlicky Stuffed Celeriac

The flesh removed from hollowed-out celeriac is mixed with garlic and parsley and replaced; the stuffed vegetables are then slowly simmered in olive oil and lemon-flavored water for extra zest.

Serves 4

INGREDIENTS
juice of 2 lemons
4 small celeriac,
    about 7–8 ounces each
⅔ cup extra virgin olive oil
lemon wedges and sprigs of fresh flat-leaf
    parsley, to garnish

FOR THE STUFFING
6 garlic cloves, finely chopped
1 teaspoon black peppercorns,
    finely crushed
4–5 tablespoons chopped
    fresh parsley
salt

2 Very carefully scoop out the flesh of each celeriac, leaving a shell about ¾ inch thick, in which to put the filling. Reserve the lemon water.

3 Working quickly, chop the scooped-out celeriac flesh and mix with the garlic and crushed peppercorns. Add the parsley and season with salt.

4 Fill the celeriac shells with the garlic stuffing and sit them in a large pan into which they fit snugly enough to remain upright throughout cooking. Pour in the olive oil and enough lemon water to come halfway up the celeriac.

1 Pour the lemon juice into a large bowl and add water until it is about two-thirds full. Peel the celeriac carefully with a sharp knife and quickly immerse in the lemon water until ready to use.

5 Simmer very gently until the celeriac are tender and nearly all the cooking liquid has been absorbed. Serve the celeriac hot or cold with their juices, and garnish with lemon wedges and sprigs of parsley.

Accordion-style Garlic Potatoes

The garlic permeates these potatoes as they bake, and they are served with an herbed cream topping.

Serves 4

INGREDIENTS
4 large baking potatoes
2 garlic cloves, cut into slivers
¼ cup sour cream
¼ cup plain yogurt
2 tablespoons snipped
    fresh chives
6–8 watercress sprigs,
    finely chopped (optional)
salt and freshly ground
    black pepper

1 Preheat the oven to 400°F. Slice each potato several times, cutting almost to the bottom, so that they retain their shape. Slip garlic slivers between some of the cuts.

2 Place the garlic-filled potatoes in a roasting pan and bake for 1–1¼ hours or until soft when tested with a knife. Meanwhile, mix the sour cream and yogurt in a bowl. Then stir in the chives along with the watercress, if using, and season to taste.

3 Serve the baked potatoes on individual plates, with a dollop of the yogurt and cream mixture on top of each one.

COOK'S TIP: The most suitable potatoes for baking are of the floury variety. Some of the best include Estima, Cara, Pentland Squire, Spunta, Kerr's Pink and Record.

Garlic Mashed Sweet Potatoes

Delicious mashed with garlicky butter, orange-fleshed sweet potatoes look attractive too.

Serves 4

INGREDIENTS
4 large sweet potatoes,
    about 2 pounds total weight, cubed
3 tablespoons unsalted butter
3 garlic cloves, crushed
salt and freshly ground black pepper

1 Cook the sweet potatoes in a large saucepan of boiling salted water for about 15 minutes or until tender, then drain and return to the pan.

COOK'S TIPS: If the sweet potatoes seem to be on the dry side when you are mashing them, add a little milk. Add some fresh chopped herbs, if desired.

2 Melt the butter in a heavy saucepan and sauté the garlic over low to medium heat for 1–2 minutes until light golden brown, stirring to prevent the garlic from burning.

3 Pour the garlic butter over the sweet potatoes and season with salt and plenty of black pepper. Mash thoroughly until smooth and creamy. Serve immediately.

Green Beans with Garlic & White Wine

Delicate and fresh-tasting small cannellini beans and garlic add a distinct French flavor to this simple side dish.

Serves 4

INGREDIENTS

1¼ cups dried small cannellini beans
1 tablespoon olive oil
2 tablespoons butter
1 onion, finely chopped
1–2 garlic cloves, crushed
3–4 tomatoes, peeled and chopped
12 ounces green beans, sliced
⅔ cup white wine
⅔ cup vegetable stock
2 tablespoons chopped fresh parsley
salt and freshly ground black pepper

1 Soak the cannellini beans in water overnight. Drain and then boil in a pan of fresh water for ¾–1 hour. Drain.

2 Heat the oil and butter in a large frying pan and sauté the onion and garlic for 3–4 minutes, until soft. Add the tomatoes and continue cooking over low heat until they are soft.

3 Stir the cannellini beans into the tomato mixture, then add the runner beans, wine, stock, and a little salt. Stir well. Cover and simmer gently for 5–10 minutes, until the green beans are tender.

4 Increase the heat to reduce the liquid, then stir in the parsley and season with a little more salt, if necessary, and pepper. Serve hot.

Stir-fried Spinach with Garlic & Sesame Seeds

Sesame seeds add a crunchy texture, and garlic brings out the flavor of the spinach in this easy vegetable dish.

Serves 2

INGREDIENTS
8 ounces fresh spinach, washed
1½ tablespoons sesame seeds
2 tablespoons peanut oil
¼ teaspoon sea salt flakes
2–3 garlic cloves, sliced

1 Shake the spinach to get rid of any excess water, then remove the stems from the leaves. Lay several leaves one on top of another, roll up tightly and cut crosswise into wide strips. Repeat with the remaining leaves.

2 Heat a wok to medium heat, add the sesame seeds and dry-fry, stirring, for 1–2 minutes, until golden brown. Transfer to a small bowl and set aside.

3 Add the oil to the wok and swirl it around. When hot, add the salt, spinach and garlic and stir-fry for 2 minutes. Sprinkle on the sesame seeds and toss well. Serve immediately.

COOK'S TIP: Take care when adding the spinach to the hot oil, as it will spit furiously.

Mushrooms in a Creamy Garlic Sauce

Fresh mint, cilantro, chiles and garlic are the prime notes in this dish, which is delicious served with plainly cooked rice.

Serves 4

INGREDIENTS
4½ cups button mushrooms
3 garlic cloves, peeled
2 fresh green chiles
3 tablespoons olive oil
1 bay leaf
1 cup fromage frais
1 tablespoon chopped fresh mint
1 tablespoon chopped cilantro
1 teaspoon salt
fresh mint and cilantro leaves,
    to garnish

3 Add the mushrooms and stir-fry briskly for about 2 minutes.

4 Remove the pan from heat and stir in the fromage frais followed by the chopped mint and cilantro. Add the salt.

1 Cut the mushrooms in half. Roughly chop the garlic. Seed and chop the chiles.

2 Heat the oil in a nonstick wok or frying pan, then add the bay leaf, garlic and chiles and cook for about 1 minute, stirring constantly.

5 Stir-fry for about 2 minutes, then transfer to a warmed serving dish. Garnish with mint and cilantro leaves and serve immediately.

Roasted Bell Pepper, Garlic & Tomato Salad

A robust garlicky dressing unites these meltingly tender vegetables.

Serves 4

INGREDIENTS
3 red bell peppers
6 large plum tomatoes
½ teaspoon dried red chile flakes
1 red onion, finely sliced
3 garlic cloves, finely chopped
grated zest and juice of 1 lemon
3 tablespoons chopped fresh flat-leaf parsley
2 tablespoons extra virgin olive oil
salt and freshly ground black pepper
black and green olives and extra chopped
   flat-leaf parsley, to garnish

1 Preheat the oven to 425°F. Place the peppers on a baking sheet and roast, turning occasionally, until the skins are almost blackened.

2 Add the tomatoes to the baking sheet and bake for 5 more minutes.

3 Place the peppers in a plastic bag, close the top loosely, trapping in the steam, and then set them aside, with the tomatoes, until they are cool.

4 Remove the skin and seeds from the peppers. Skin the tomatoes, then chop the peppers and tomatoes roughly and place in a mixing bowl.

5 Add the chile flakes, onion, garlic, lemon zest and juice. Sprinkle on the parsley. Mix well, then transfer to a serving dish. Sprinkle with a little salt, drizzle on the olive oil and sprinkle olives and extra parsley on top.

Spinach & Roasted Garlic Salad with Pine Nuts

Sweet and subtle-tasting roasted garlic makes this simple dish memorable.

Serves 4

INGREDIENTS
12 garlic cloves, unpeeled
¼ cup extra virgin olive oil
1 pound baby spinach leaves
½ cup pine nuts, lightly toasted
juice of ½ lemon
salt and freshly ground black pepper

1 Preheat the oven to 375°F. Place the garlic in a small roasting dish, toss in 2 tablespoons of the olive oil and bake for about 15 minutes, until the garlic cloves are slightly charred around the edges.

2 While still warm, transfer the garlic to a salad bowl. Add the spinach, pine nuts, lemon juice, remaining olive oil and a little salt. Toss well and add black pepper to taste.

3 Serve immediately, inviting guests to squeeze the softened garlic purée out of the skin to eat.

COOK'S TIP: If spinach is to be served raw in a salad, the leaves need to be young and tender. Wash them well, drain and pat dry with paper towels.

This edition published by Southwater

Distributed in the UK by
The Manning Partnership,
251–253 London Road East, Batheaston,
Bath BA1 7RL, UK
tel. (0044) 01225 852 727
fax. (0044) 01225 852 852

Distributed in New Zealand by
Five Mile Press NZ,
PO Box 33–1071, Takapuna
Auckland 9, New Zealand
tel. (0064) 9 4444 144
fax. (0064) 9 4444 518

Distributed in Australia by
Sandstone Publishing,
Unit 1, 360 Norton Street, Leichhardt,
New South Wales 2040, Australia
tel. (0061) 2 9560 7888
fax. (0061) 2 9560 7488

Southwater is an imprint of Anness Publishing Limited

© 2000 Anness Publishing Limited

Publisher: Joanna Lorenz
Editor: Valerie Ferguson
Series Designer: Bobbie Colgate Stone
Designer: Andrew Heath
Production Controller: Joanna King

1 3 5 7 9 10 8 6 4 2

Printed and bound in Singapore

Recipes contributed by: Catherine Atkinson,
Michelle Berriedale-Johnson, Angela Boggiano,
Carla Capalbo, Jacqueline Clark, Carole Clements,
Trish Davis, Matthew Drennan, Sarah Edmonds,
Silvano Franco, Shirley Gill, Nicola Graimes,
Shehzad Husain, Christine Ingram, Lesley Mackley,
Norma Miller, Sallie Morris, Maggie Pannell,
Liz Trigg, Steven Wheeler, Elizabeth Wolf-Cohen,
Jeni Wright.

Photography: William Adams-Lingwood,
Karl Adamson, James Duncan, Joanna Farrow,
Ian Garlick, Michelle Garrett, Kathryn Hawkins,
Amanda Heywood, Ferguson Hill,
Janine Hosegood, David Jordan, Patrick McLeavey,
Thomas Odulate.